Pebble® Plus

Aircraft

Seaplanes

by Mari Schuh

Consulting Editor: Gail Saunders-Smith, PhD

Consultant: Stewart W. Bailey, Curator
Evergreen Aviation & Space Museum
McMinnville, Oregon

CAPSTONE PRESS
a capstone imprint

Pebble Plus is published by Capstone Press,
1710 Roe Crest Drive, North Mankato, Minnesota 56003
www.capstonepub.com

Library of Congress Cataloging-in-Publication Data
Cataloging-in-publication information is on file with the Library of Congress.
978-1-62065-114-8 (library binding)
978-1-4765-1071-2 (eBook PDF)

Editorial Credits
Erika L. Shores, editor; Heidi Thompson, designer; Eric Manske, production specialist

Photo Credits
Alamy: Stockfolio®, 17; Corbis: JAI/John Warburton-Lee, 7, Robert Garvey, 21, Transtock, 19; Dreamstime: Henryike, cover;
National Geographic Stock: Alaska Stock Images, 5; Newscom: A3724 Felix Heyder Deutsch Presse Agentur, 11, Danita
Delimont Photography/Ralph H. Bendjebar, 13; Shutterstock: Bruce L. Crandall, 9, Dimitriadi Kharlampiy, 15

Artistic Effects
Shutterstock: New Line

The author dedicates this book to the Krizek family of Racine, Wisconsin.

Note to Parents and Teachers

The Aircraft set supports national science standards related to science, technology, and society.
This book describes and illustrates seaplanes. The images support early readers in understanding
the text. The repetition of words and phrases helps early readers learn new words. This book also
introduces early readers to subject-specific vocabulary words, which are defined in the Glossary
section. Early readers may need assistance to read some words and to use the Table of Contents,
Glossary, Read More, Internet Sites, and Index sections of the book.

Printed in China
092012   006934LEOS13

Table of Contents

Seaplanes

Splash! A seaplane makes
a landing. These airplanes
can land and float
on water. They can take off
from the water too.

Seaplanes can land in areas

that are hard to reach.

Runways can't be built

in some places. Cars and trains

can't reach other spots.

N67112

Valhalla

Kinds of Seaplanes

What are the different kinds of seaplanes? A floatplane doesn't have wheels. It skims across the water on floats. Floats look like long water skis.

Flying boats have a big body.

The plane's body floats

in the water like a ship.

Amphibian planes can
land and take off from
runways and from water.

Amphibian planes have

wheels that can hide away.

Pilots use the wheels on land.

They raise the wheels when

the plane is in water.

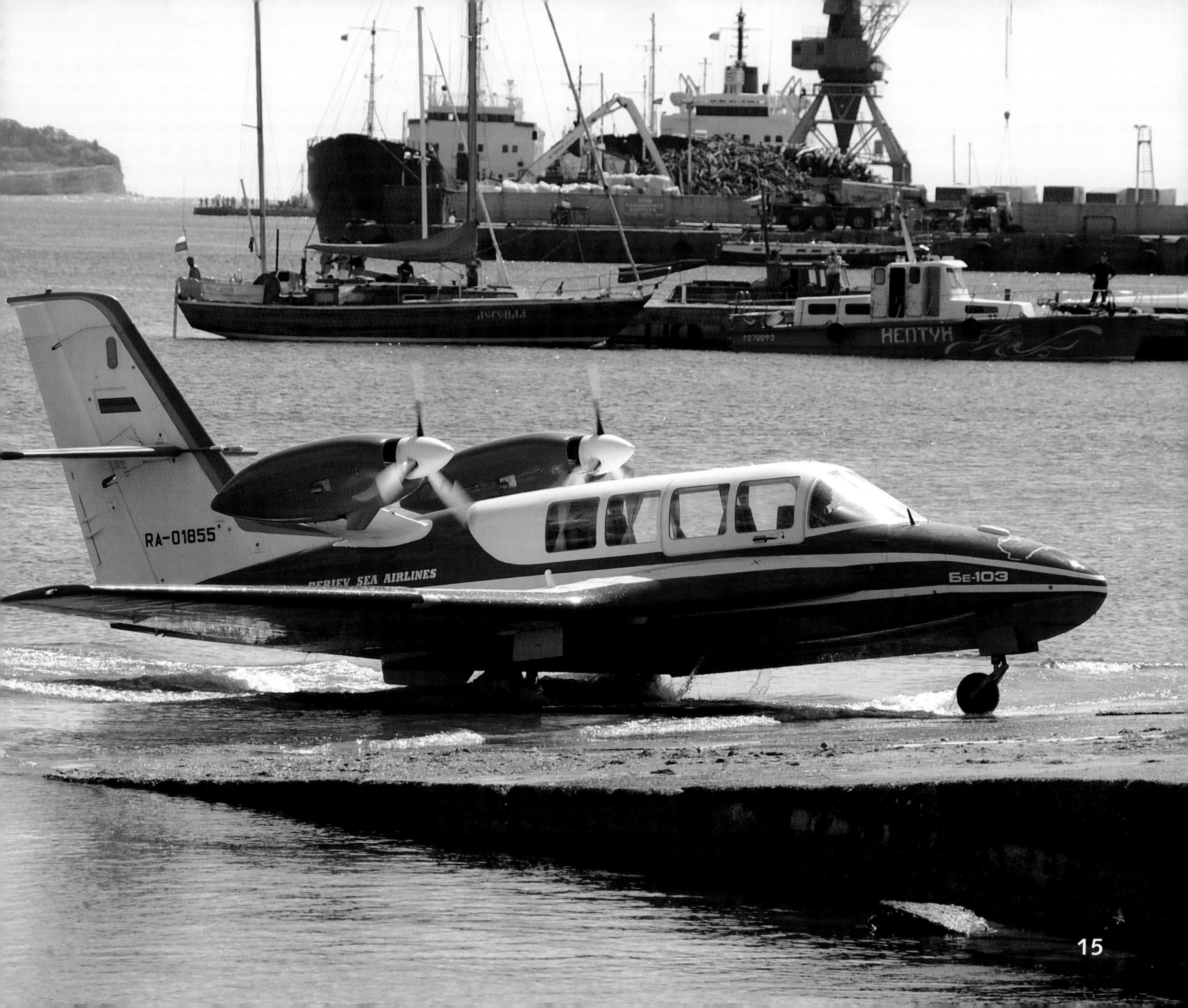
RA-01855
BERIEV SEA AIRLINES
Бе-103
НЕПТУН

What Seaplanes Do

Fire-fighting seaplanes scoop water from lakes and oceans. A "Superscooper" fills its tank in 12 seconds. Then it dumps the water on forest fires.

17

Seaplanes search for
missing boats and ships.
Seaplanes rescue
people in trouble.

Up, Up, and Away!

The engine revs as a seaplane

skims across water.

Soon the plane is high

in the sky.

Glossary

amphibian plane—a plane that can land and take off from both water and land

engine—a machine that makes the power to move something

float—to rest on water or air; a float is a long part on a seaplane that allows the plane to safely land on water

pilot—the person who flies airplanes or other aircraft

rescue—to save someone who is danger

runway—an area of flat land that airplanes use to take off and land

Read More

Dos Santos, Julie. *Aircraft.* Amazing Machines. Tarrytown, N.Y.: Marshall Cavendish Benchmark, 2010.

Hanson, Anders. *Let's Go By Airplane.* Let's Go! Edina, Minn.: ABDO, 2008.

Riehle, Mary Ann McCabe. *A Is For Airplane: An Aviation Alphabet.* Chelsea, Mich.: Sleeping Bear Press, 2009.

Internet Sites

FactHound offers a safe, fun way to find Internet sites related to this book. All of the sites on FactHound have been researched by our staff.

Here's all you do:

Visit *www.facthound.com*

Type in this code: 9781620651148

Super-cool stuff!   Check out projects, games and lots more at **www.capstonekids.com**

Index

Word Count: 176
Grade: 1
Early-Intervention Level: 18